Alta, d

Kjære Meredith,

Det var hyggelig at du ville komme
hit nord og feire jul sammens med
oss.

Go tur videre i verden, og velkommen
tilbake.

Gerd og Harald

North

Look North more often.

Go against the wind, you'll get ruddy cheeks.

Find the rough path. Keep to it.

It's shorter.

North is best.

Winter's flaming sky, summer-

night's sun miracle.

Go against the wind. Climb mountains.

Look north.

More often.

This land is long.

Most is north.

Rolf Jacobsen
(Trans. Olav Grinde)

Just thin needles -
It's so thin, the light.
And there is so little of it.

Darkness is vast.
Light is only thin needles
in endless night.

And it has to travel so far

through desolate space.

So let us be gentle with it.

Cherish it.

So that it will return tomorrow.

Let's hope.

Rolf Jacobsen, (Trans. Olav Grinde)

Life is strange
When everything is meaningless
it is as if one dreamed
a nightmare

And when the sun warms
all of life's work
all is like a dream

Nils-Aslak Valkeapää

On frost-green sky over mountain peaks, play

tongues of fire.

Night of longing.

Night of sun.

Flickering searchlights probe restlessly

inwards - inwards

to the endless, unplumbed spaces.

Jan Magnus Bruheim

Oh, still to sing of midsummer nights,

and still to breathe the soft spiced air,

still to know all the flowers by sight

and name them by colour and scent so fair.

Still to be a soul which in dreaming

boldly eternal thoughts sends streaming

beyond the ether and reason's sway . . .

Herman Wildenvey

Midsummer night

Sit in reverie and watch
the changing color of the waves
that break upon
the idle seashores of the mind.

H.W.Longfellow

Morning mood

If the sight of the blue skies fills you with joy,

if a blade of grass springing up in the fields

has power to move you,

if the simple things of nature

have a message you understand,

rejoice, for your soul is alive.

Eleanora Duse

The brightness of a June evening
is like a little sparrow's
play in clean water

where it splashes off
the cares of the world and soars
jubilant into the air

giddy with summer's purity!

Gunvor Hofmo

Summer night over Bleik

To the north the grey geese are flocking
to the land where fables are spun,
where the day lies quietly dreaming
in the pale fire of the midnight sun.

Vilhelm Krag

Butterflies

From secret paths butterflies take wing:

moments igniting in glowing colour,

mysteries that flutter away and quick as a flash hide

past, future, intimations suddenly aroused.

God's presence opens fleetingly to your senses,

beauty trembles a second in outspread repose.

Life darts through you all at once - you dance.

The moment hovers, the heart is visited by a timeless smile.

Harald Sverdrup

Nesting cliff, Ekkerøy

And flocks of seabirds here in the north
flowers of the air become
and new-formed lies the land of hope
in the wondrous midnight sun

Nordahl Grieg

Morning air is like froth on the waves.

Day takes pleasure in balmy ease.

Evening has peace.

But only night holds the universe.

André Bjerke

Now.
Such a tiny word.
Now.
And yet it holds
all eternity.

Hans Børli
(Trans. Olav Grinde)

I like the night. It's as if night had no right to exist.

People are always harping on about the beauty of the sun and the day.

They're a delight to the eye and soul, that's true.

But there are hidden rooms in us the sunlight never reaches

but where only the night dare creep in.

Sigbjørn Obstfelder

Summer night on Andøy

Now shakes loose the sun its golden mane
in the morning's early hours
and spreads it out over the spring-bright plain
where bloom a thousand flowers.

Pär Lagerkvist

Warm

You are warm

Sun shy morning red

but warm

The sea smells of salt

An outbound boat disappears

Morning is the time of vision

Morning sea

a promise of future

Nils-Aslak Valkeapää

I am darkness. Darkness
that makes a thousand swaying lights
shine so painfully clearly.

I love those burning lights,
love the flame

that lies down
and trembles ecstatically before
the breath of night. I want to be

alive like that flame, but
I am darkness
that makes those lights shine.

Hans Børli, (Trans. Olav Grinde)

Lovund and Træna in the midnight sun

Owner of the moment
What more can you own

You, the first-born
You child of the Everlasting

The moment
The first cause

The moment   *Here stands the sun*   *Here is born*

Without horizons   *unmoving in the heavens*   *the everlasting Word*

Arnold Eidslott

If a light beckons to you, follow it. If it leads you into the quagmire, you'll probably find your way out of it again; but if you don't follow it, you'll be plagued for the rest of your life by the thought that perhaps it was your star.

Friedrich Hebbel

I listen

anew:

spring-sounds in my ears grow

lighter.

And sounds are no longer

sounds only

but also light

endless days . . .

B. Moske

Dried fish on Lofoten

Completorium

In the evening

to enter

a cathedral

to be alone

together with all the others

who are alone

gathered together

quite still

to reach

by thought's flickering light

the darkness

deep within us.

Olga Egeland

Humpback whale

Midnight sun

snares

night-sleep

in golden

lasso

shows off its

star turn

to the time-bemused

Olava Bidtnes

I saw that it was beautiful:

The black and gray mountains,

majestic ebony and silver.

A silk-screened image

against a luminous sky.

Liv Lundberg, (trans. Susan Schwartz Senstad)

Frosted window

Star-swarm!

Look, there's frost on the window. It is the stars

crackling like frozen dew on Earth's window.

Let's breathe on them,

extend our heart's sign,

our young warmth to the sleeping crystals,

so they turn to tears of joy, smilingly

stream away, and allow us

a glimpse of storm-blue sky.

Rolf Jacobsen, (Trans. Olav Grinde)

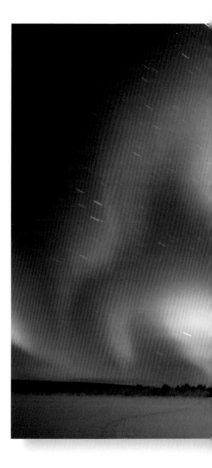

NORTHERN LIGHTS AND MIDNIGHT SUN

Text and pictures: Jens-Uwe Kumpch, Snorre Aske, E.Fraser
Idea and layout: Natur og Kulturforlaget AS

Rolf Jacobsen: North (introduction) and Frosted Window (p. 47), in Night Open,
Selected Poems of Rolf Jacobsen, White Pine Press, Fredonia/New York 1993
Bare tynne nåler (p. 3), trans. Olav Grinde, from: Pusteøvelse, Gyldendal 1975

Nils-Aslak Valkeapää (p. 5 and 31): "Trekways of the wind" (excerpt), trans. Ralph Salisbury,
L. Nordström and H. Gaski, Forlaget DAT, Guovdageaidnu 1994.

Jan-Magnus Bruheim: Brevet til kjærligheten (excerpt), trans. E. Fraser, Aschehoug 1977

Herman Wildenvey: O, ennu å være ...(excerpt), trans. E. Fraser, from: Mine sangers bok, Gyldendal 3:1996

Gunvor Hofmo: Juninatt (excerpt), trans. E. Fraser, in Ord til bilder, from: Samlede dikt, Gyldendal 1996

Harald Sverdrup: Sommerfugler, trans. E. Fraser, from Isbjørnfantasi, Aschehoug 1961

André Bjerke: Natten, trans. E. Fraser, from: Syngende jord, Aschehoug 1940

Hans Børli: (p. 25) Nå, trans. Olav Grinde, from: På harmonikk, Aschehoug 1991
(p. 33) Jeg er mørket, trans. Olav Grinde, from: Brønnen utenfor Nachors stad, Aschehoug 1966

Pär Lagerkvist, trans. E. Fraser, in: Göran Hassler: Ordens musikk, en antologi, Litteraturfrämjandet 1990

Arnold Eidslott: Ouverture, trans. E. Fraser, in Det forlatte øyeblikk from: A. Eidslott: Dikt i utvalg,
red. Jan Inge Sørbø, Gyldendal 1991

B. Moske: I ura vil jeg gjømme (excerpt), trans. E. Fraser, from: H. Gaski: Våja våja nana nana,
Cappelen 1991

Olga Egeland: Kompletorium, trans. E. Fraser, from: Miniatyrer, Aschehoug 1973

Olava Bidtnes: Midnattsolen, trans. E. Fraser, from Iren Reppen (red.): Nordnorsk temperament,
Kagge 2001

Liv Lundberg: Skjønnhet og slit (excerpt), trans. Susan Schwartz Senstad, from: Ny nordnorsk lyrikk,
Tiden 1978

Photographs: www.nettfoto.no, omslag og s. 7, 9, 11, 17, 27, 31, 33, 37, 39, 41, 45, Jørn B. Olsen / Rolf Sørensen /NN/ Samfoto, s.3, Arvid Sveen s. 5, Tore Wuttudal /NN/ Samfoto s. 13, Bård Løken /NN/ Samfoto s. 15, 29, Bjørn Erik Olsen s. 19, Pål Hermansen /NN/ Samfoto s. 21, Jorma Lutha s. 23, Asgeir Helgestad /NN/ Samfoto s. 25, Øystein Søbye /NN/ Samfoto s. 35, Alaskastock s. 43, www.Naturfoto.se s. 47.